Accountant Jokes

The Ultimate Collection of Accountancy Jokes

C000163875

Jokes For Accountants

These jokes for accountants will make you giggle. Some of these jokes are old, some of them are new and we hope you enjoy this bumper collection of the very best accountancy jokes and puns around.

In this book you will find many accountant jokes that will hopefully make you laugh. We've got some great one-liners to start with, plenty of quick fire question and answer themed gags, some story led jokes and as a bonus some cheesy pick-up lines for accountants.

This mixture of accountancy jokes is guaranteed to get you laughing.

Published by Glowworm Press
7 Nuffield Way
Abingdon OX14 1RL

FOREWORD

When I was asked to write a foreword to this book I was very flattered.

That is until I was told that I was the last resort by the author, Chester Croker, and that everyone else he had approached had said they couldn't do it!

I have known Chester for a number of years and his ability to create funny jokes is absolutely incredible. He is quick witted and an expert at crafting clever puns and amusing gags and I feel he is the ideal man to put together a joke book about our number crunching profession as he once told me it's accrual world.

He will be glad you have bought this book, as he has an expensive lifestyle to maintain.

Enjoy!

Penny Wise

Table of Contents

Chapter 1: One-Liner Accountant Jokes

During my induction at one of the big four accounting firms, I was told, "Welcome to the accounting department, where everybody counts."

A fine is a tax for doing wrong and a tax is a fine for doing well.

I might be certified, but I'm not crazy.

Accountants don't die, they just get de-recognized.

A tax accountant makes a better detective than Sherlock Holmes, since accountants make more deductions.

A budget is an orderly system for living beyond your means.

Accounting for Dummies: What's the big deal? It's simply Cr. Cash Dr. Dummies.

You might be a tax accountant if you refer to your youngest child as Deduction 214.

My financial accountant told me that the only reason my business is looking up is because it is flat on its back.

Conversation overheard between two accountants at a cocktail party, "And ninthly…"

Accountants always laugh out loud when somebody asks for a raise.

The accountant crossed the road because she looked in the files and did what they did last year.

When accountants take out a loan they become very debticated.

There are just three types of accountants: those who can count and those who can't.

You might be an accountant if you decide to change your name to a symbol and you choose the double underline.

An accountant is someone who knows the cost of everything and the value of nothing.

The last day of the month is our favourite day of the month to work in the finance business said no employee ever.

Few of us ever test our powers of deduction, except when we are filling out an income tax form.

A fine is a tax for doing the accounts wrong. A tax is a fine for doing the accounts well.

The time is 4:04 but do you know where your accountant is?

You might be an accountant if you did a NPV calculation while watching the Indecent Proposal movie.

My Finance Director once told me, "For every tax problem there is a solution that is straightforward, uncomplicated, and wrong."

My senior accountant explained to me why it is called Form 1040. For every $50 you earn, you get $10, they get $40.

A good accountant never makes misteaks.

Did you hear about the cross eyed accountant? He had to quit because he couldn't see eye to eye with his clients.

An accountants best defence is that they are not really boring people, they just get excited over boring things.

I got called pretty today. Actually, the full sentence was "You're a pretty bad accountant." but I'm choosing to focus on the positive.

Did you hear about the deviant forensic accountant? He got his client's charges reduced from gross indecency to net indecency.

Materiality in accounts depends on the audit deadline.

Definition of an accountant: A person who only has an opinion once you pay them.

You might well be an accountant if you have no idea that GAP is also a clothing brand.

Yesterday, an accountant's wife asked to be passed her lipstick. He passed her a stick of super-glue by mistake. She isn't talking to him now.

Accountancy words of wisdom: - The splendour of a company's office decor varies inversely with the fundamental solvency of the firm.

A lesson learnt from many years accountancy is that creditors have far better memories than debtors.

I'm not sure whether to laugh or cry after my meeting with my accountant today. He took one look at my files and retired.

Two things in life are inevitable: death and taxes. At least death only happens once.

Definition of an accountant: A person who solves a problem you didn't know you had in a way you don't understand.

I'm on the audit report diet. I've lost three days already.

Did you hear about the Irish management accountant? She went to see her fitness trainer to talk about stretch targets.

Definition of an accountant: A person who does precision guesswork based on unreliable data provided by those of questionable knowledge.

Did you hear about the constipated junior accountant? He couldn't budget with his calculator so he had to work it out with a pencil and paper.

My FD once told me, "Finance is the art of passing currency from hand to hand until it finally disappears."

Did you hear about the accountancy practice run by cannibals?

They charge their clients an arm and a leg.

The most successful CFO was Noah. He floated stock, while everything around him went into liquidation.

Our Finance Director was quoted at the last board meeting as saying, "We didn't actually overspend our budget. The allocation simply fell short of our expenditure."

Did you hear about the work shy accountant who ran out of sick days so he called in dead.

My senior accountant once told me, "A bargain is something you can't use at a price you can't resist."

A good accountant is a debit to the profession.

Did you hear about the fraudulent accountant? He burned his office down trying to cook the books.

An economist is someone who didn't have enough personality to become an accountant.

Did you hear about the trainee accountant who stole a calendar? He got twelve months.

An accountant couldn't get to sleep so he started counting sheep. He made a mistake and it took him three hours trying to find it.

An accountant laughs loudest when it's at someone else's expense.

Chapter 2: Q&A Accountant Jokes

Q: What happened when an accountant crossed a chili pepper, a shovel and a Yorkshire terrier?

A: *He got a hot-diggity-dog.*

Q: How does an accountant stay out of debt?

A: *He learns to act his wage.*

Q: What do accountants do for fun?

A: *Add up the numbers in the telephone book.*

Q: Do accountants ever laugh out loud?

A: *It depends on their clients.*

Q: Why do accountants make good lovers?

A: *They are great with figures.*

Q: What does an accountant say when you ask him the time?

A: *It's 11.18 am and 15 seconds; no, wait – 16 seconds; no wait – 17 seconds; no wait...*

Q: What does an accountant say when boarding a train?

A: *Mind the GAAP.*

Q: What is the definition of an accountant?

A: *Someone who solves a problem you didn't know you had in a way you don't understand.*

Q: How does an Accountant pray?

A: *Lord, please help me be more relaxed about insignificant details, starting tomorrow at 8:57 a.m. Eastern Daylight Savings time.*

Q: What do you call an accountant without a calculator?

A: *Lonely*.

Q: Why did God invent economists?

A: *So accountants could have someone to laugh at.*

Q: What's the difference between an accountant and a lawyer?

A: *The accountant knows he's boring.*

Q: If an accountant's wife cannot sleep, what does she say?

A: *"Darling, could you tell me about your work?"*

Q: How does Santa's accountant value his sleigh?

A: *Net Present Value.*

Q: Why was the accountant in rehab?

A: *For solvency abuse.*

Q: When does a person decide to become an accountant?

A: *When they realize they don't have the charisma to succeed as undertakers.*

Q: How do old accountants die?

A: *They just lose their balance.*

Q: Why does Santa like visiting the UK?

A: *He can claim Gift Relief.*

Q: Did you hear about the triple – entry bookkeeping used by some accountants in the 1990s?

A: *Debit, credit and shred – it.*

Q: What music is played at an accountant's leaving party?

A: *The Last Post.*

Q: What does CPA stand for?

A: *Can't Pass Again.*

Q: Why do accountants suffer from, that ordinary people don't?

A: *Depreciation.*

Q: What's an accountant's favorite book?

A: *50 Shades of Grey.*

Q: How many accountants does it take to change a light bulb?

A: *How much money do you have?*

Q: What's a shy and retiring accountant?

A: *One that's half a million shy and that's why he's retiring.*

Q: What do you call a trial balance that doesn't balance?

A: *A late night.*

Q: Why did the cannibal accountant get reprimanded?

A: *For buttering up her clients.*

Q: Why did the auditor cross the road?

A: *To bore the people on the other side.*

Q: What do you call an accountant without a spread sheet?

A: *Lost.*

Q: How can you tell when the chief accountant is getting soft?

A: *When he actually listens to marketing before saying no.*

Q: Which clients do short accountants like best?

A: *Small businesses.*

Q: How can you drive an accountant crazy?

A: *Stand in front of him and fold up a road map the wrong way.*

Q: How do accountants make a bold fashion statement?

A: *They wear their dark grey socks instead of the light grey.*

Q: What's the definition of a very good tax accountant?

A: *Someone who has a loophole named after him.*

Q: Why don't accountants read novels?

A: *Because the only numbers in them are the page numbers.*

Q: Why did the auditor get run over crossing the road?

A: *Auditors never do a risk assessment until after an accident has happened.*

Q: Where do homeless accountants live?

A: *In tax shelters.*

Q: How does an accountant trash their hotel room?

A: *By refusing to fill in the Guest Comment Card.*

Q: What did the accountant say when he got a blank check?

A: *My deductions have at last caught up with my salary.*

Q: When does a person decide to become an accountant?

A: *When he realizes he has less charisma than an undertaker.*

Q: What do you call an accountant who is happy every Monday morning?

A: *Retired.*

Q: When do accountants get upset?

A: *When they lose their balance.*

Q: What happens when you put a wild hyena in a room with an internal auditor?

A: *The hyena stops laughing.*

Q: How does a CPA say the F-word?

A: *Trust Me.*

Q: What do accountants suffer from, that most people don't?

A: *Depreciation.*

Q: What does a CFO use for birth control?

A: *His personality.*

Q: When is an accountant's smile the widest?

A: *The day their bill gets paid.*

Q: Why do accountants get excited at the weekends?

A: *Because they can wear casual clothes to work.*

Q: How do you know when an accountant is on holiday?

A: *He doesn't wear a tie and comes in after 8am!*

Q: Why are accountants always so calm, composed, and methodical?

A: *They have strong internal controls.*

Q: What do you call an accountant without a spreadsheet?

A: *Lost.*

Chapter 3: Short Accountant Jokes

The senior accountant walks into his boss's office and says, "The auditors have just left, sir."

"Have they finished checking the books?" asks the boss.

"Very thoroughly," comes the reply.

"Well, what did they say?" says the boss.

"They want 12% to keep quiet," says the senior accountant.

The first accountant on earth was Adam.

He was interested in figures, turned the first leaf, made the first entry, lost interest after withdrawal, messed up the monthly accounts and raised the first liability.

Two young accountants were walking in the park when one said, "Where did you get your bike?"

The second accountant replied, "Well, yesterday I was walking along the road minding my own business when an attractive woman rode up on this bike.

She threw the bike to the ground, quickly took off all her clothes and said, "Take what you want from me."

The first accountant nodded approvingly, "That was a good choice as the clothes probably wouldn't have fitted you very well."

An accountant reads a nursery rhyme to his young son and then answers his child's question by saying, "No son, after Little Bo Peep has lost her sheep, they are not tax deductible. But I like your thinking."

An accountant goes to his doctor as he is suffering with a hearing problem.

The doctor says, "Can you describe the symptoms to me?"

The accountant replies, "Yes. Homer is a lazy fat yellow and his wife Marge is skinny with big blue hair."

An accountant is talking to a young daughter of one of his friends and he asks her, "Do you know what I do?'

The girl replies, "Daddy says you're a CPA."

The accountant asks, "That's right. Did he tell you what CPA stands for?"

The girl replies, "Yes, he said you're a complete pain in the a***."

An accountant meets his blonde girlfriend as she's picking up her car from the mechanic.

"Everything ok with your car now?" he asks.

"Yes, thank goodness," the dizzy blonde replies.

He asks, "Weren't you worried the mechanic might try to rip you off?"

She replies, "Yes, but he didn't. I was so relieved when he told me that all I needed was blinker fluid!"

My accountant friend went to his doctor and told him he was covered in a rash.

The doctor examined him thoroughly and then declared, "As I suspected – it's ticks."

An accountant tries to enter a smart cocktail bar wearing a shirt open at the collar, and is met by a doorman who denies him entry saying he must wear a necktie to gain admission.

The accountant goes back to his car as he knows he has some jump leads in his boot; and he gets them out and creates a knot by tying them around his neck, and he lets the cable ends dangle free.

He goes back to the bar and the doorman looks him over very carefully, and then declares, "Well, I guess you can come in - just don't start anything."

An aspiring businessman goes to the senior accountant of a company for advice and asks, "How do I start a small business?"

The senior accountant replies, "Start a large one and give it six months."

An accountant is in a car travelling with a farmer client around his farm.

They pass a large flock of sheep and the farmer says, "You think you're good with numbers don't you? Well, just how many sheep do you think are in that paddock?"

The accountant looks at the sheep for a while and then says, "Two hundred and seven."

The farmer is stunned. "You are exactly right," he says, "how did you work that out so quickly?"

"Easy," says the accountant, "I simply counted the number of feet and divided by four."

A husband and wife are watching their young son playing.

She says, "He is such a sensitive child. Let's wait until he is older before we tell him you are an accountant."

A team of accountants was working late finishing off a year-end audit for a large consultancy firm.

A cleaner had just finished washing the floor when one of the accountants asked to use the toilet.

With dismay the cleaner looked at the newly polished floor.

"Just a minute," she said, "I'll put down some newspaper."

"That's all right, madam," he responded. "I'm house trained."

Everybody is asking themselves why the accountant started smoking.

The answer was right before their eyes.

It was so that he could deduct cigarettes from his income tax.

He called it loss by fire so his medical expenses went above the 7 1/2% threshold.

It's Halloween and when the home owner answers his front door, he sees a young boy wearing a suit and matching tie, who says, "Trick or treat."

The home owner is a little confused so he asks the boy what he's dressed up as.

"I'm an IRS agent," says the boy, and with that, he snatches 40% of the candy, and leaves without saying thank you.

An accountant is late for a meeting and is unable to find a parking spot.

"Lord," he said out loud. "I can't cope. If you open a space up for me, I swear I'll give up the booze and go to church every Sunday."

Suddenly, the clouds part and the sun shines down onto an empty parking space.

Without hesitation, the accountant says, "Never mind Lord, I've found a spot."

One day in microeconomics class, the professor was writing up the typical "underlying assumptions" in preparation to explain a new model to the students.

One student turned to his friend and asked, "What would Economics be without assumptions?"

He thought for a few seconds and then replied, "Accounting."

A proud father is showing pictures of his three sons to an old friend he hasn't seen for a while, and his friend asked him, "What do your boys do for a living?"

He replied, "Well my youngest is a neurosurgeon and my middle is a lawyer."

"What does the oldest child do?" his friend asked.

The reply came, "He's the accountant that paid for the others' education."

The managing partner in an accounting firm is very annoyed with one of his junior partners and has called him in to chastise him.

He says, "How could you possibly advise the client in the way that you did? That was completely unethical. We are always conscious of ethics in this firm. You do know what ethics is don't you?"

The young partner is offended and replies, "Of course I know what ethics is. It's a county in southern England."

A dog walks into a bar, sits down and says to the barman, "Can I have a pint of lager and a packet of crisps please."

The barman who had not heard a talking dog before says, "Wow, that's incredible; you should join the circus."

The dog replies, "Why? Do they need accountants?"

An accountant had just read the bed time story of Cinderella to his four year-old daughter for the first time.

The girl was completely absorbed by the story, especially the part where the pumpkin turns into a golden coach.

Showing her family traits, she asked her father, "When the pumpkin turned into a golden coach, would that be classed as income or a capital gain?"

An accountant had a roofer called Gary working on his house repairing some tiles.

Gary is up on the roof and accidentally cuts off his ear, and he shouts down to the accountant, "Hey. Look out for my ear I just cut off."

The accountant picks something up and shouts up to the roofer, "Is this your ear?"

Gary looks down and says, "Nope. Mine had a pencil behind it!"

An accountant complained to his close friend that his wife of twenty years didn't satisfy him anymore.

His friend advised him to find another woman on the side, pretty sharpish.

When they met up a month or so later, the accountant told his buddy, "I took your advice. I managed to find a woman on the side, but my wife still doesn't satisfy me!"

An IRS agent was walking through a park on his lunch break when a mugger leapt from behind a bush and demanded, "Give me all of your money."

The IRS agent said, "You can't do that - I work for the IRS."

"In that case," said the mugger, "Give me all of MY money!"

An accountant took his cross-eyed labrador along to the vet.

The vet picked the dog up to examine him and said, "Sorry, I'm going to have to put him down."

The accountant said, "Oh no! It's not that bad is it?"

The vet replied, "No, he's just very heavy."

An accountant in my area went to jail for dealing drugs.

I've been one of his customers for over six years, and yet I had no clue that he was an accountant.

Newton's Laws of Accounting

1. For every accountant, there is an equal and opposite accountant.
2. Both of them are wrong.

Two senior accountants are talking about sex.

The first says that sex is 75% work and 25% pleasure.

The second says that sex is 25% work and 75% pleasure.

At a standstill, they decide to ask their trainee for his opinion.

"Sex is all pleasure." says the trainee.

"Why do you say that?" ask the senior accountants.

The trainee replies, "Simple. If there is any work involved, you two make me do it."

Nowadays it is easy to spot popular accountants from the ones that are unpopular.

All you need to do is find the accountant who is seen talking to someone who isn't also an accountant.

A farmer sends his border collie off to gather in his 48 sheep.

On returning the farmer is amazed to find that there are now 50 sheep in the pen so he asks the dog to explain.

"Woof. You told me to round them up, woof, woof", barks his dog.

A woman went to the doctor who told her that she only had a year to live.

The woman exclaimed, "What shall I do?"

"Marry an accountant," suggested the doctor.

"Why?" asked the woman. "Will that make me live longer?"

"No," replied the doctor. "But it will seem longer."

You will understand this book if you can ask yourself one particular question at the most particular time.

At exactly 4:04, do you know where your accountant is?

There are two rules for creating and running a successful accountancy business:-

1. Don't tell your clients everything you know.

2. [Redacted]

A company director hires a private detective to find a missing accountant.

The detective tells him he needs a description and he asks, "Was he tall or was he short?"

The director replies, "Both."

An old accountant was walking along the road one day when he came across a frog.

He reached down, picked the frog up, and started to put it in his pocket. As he did so, the frog said, "Kiss me on the lips and I'll turn into a beautiful woman."

The old accountant carried on putting the frog in his pocket.

The frog said, "Didn't you hear what I said?"

The accountant looked at the frog and said, "Yes, but at my age I'd rather have a talking frog."

An IRS agent is lying on his psychiatrist's couch protesting that everyone in the world hates him.

"Baloney", says his doctor. "That is simply not the case. Everyone in the world does not hate you."

He continues, "Everyone in the US, probably, but definitely not everyone in the world."

An accountant took his son to the Natural History Museum. While standing near one of the dinosaurs he said to his son, "This dinosaur is two billion years and ten months old."

The son asked, "Where did you get this exact information?"

The accountant replied, "I was here ten months ago, and the guide told me that the dinosaur is two billion years old."

American military experts were discussing the Six Day War with an Israeli general, and they were keen to know how it had ended so quickly.

The general told them, "We had a crack regiment at the most strategically important front. It was made entirely of lawyers and accountants. When the time came to charge - boy, did they know how to charge."

An accountant and a lawyer were lying on hotel loungers in Hawaii sipping cocktails.

The lawyer started to tell the accountant how he came to be there.

He said, "I had this downtown property in Chicago that caught fire and after the insurance paid off, I came here."

The accountant raised his eyebrows and said, "I had a downtown property in Miami. It got flooded so here I am with the insurance proceeds."

The lawyer took another sip of his Mai Tai, and then asked the accountant in a puzzled voice, "Just how do you start a flood?"

A woman from HR quizzed an accountant saying, "Did you call an employee stupid?"

The accountant replied, "No, I asked if he was stupid!"

A business owner tells his friend that he is urgently searching for a good accountant.

His friend enquires, "Didn't your company hire an accountant just a few weeks ago?"

The business owner replies, "Yes, he's the accountant I am searching for."

An accountant says to his boss, "Here is this month's financial report."

The CFO replies, "Good job. However, the budget has now changed. We need you to re-do the whole thing."

Chapter 4: Longer Accountant Jokes

Three Friends

Ron is talking to two of his friends, Jim and Shamus.

Jim says, "I think my wife is having an affair with an accountant. The other day I came home and found a calculator under our bed and it wasn't mine."

Shamus then confides, "Wow, me too! I think my wife is having an affair with an auditor. The other day I found wire cutters under the bed and they weren't mine."

Ron thinks for a minute and then says, "You know - I think my wife is having an affair with a horse."

Both Jim and Shamus look at him in complete disbelief.

Ron sees them looking at him and says, "No, seriously. The other day I came home early and found a jockey under our bed."

St. Peter and the Accountant

An accountant dies from a heart attack and goes to heaven.

St. Peter is there, looking through the files and asks, "What sort of accountant were you?"

"Oh, I was a CPA", was the reply.

"What is your name?" asks St. Peter.

The accountant gives his name and St. Peter finds his file.

"Oh yes, we've been expecting you. You've reached your allotted time span."

The accountant says, "I don't get it. How can that be? I'm only 54 years old."

St. Peter looks again at the file and says, "Well, that's impossible."

"Why do you say that?" asks the accountant.

"Well," says St. Peter, "we've been looking over your time sheets and the hours you've charged your clients. By our reckoning, you must be at least 95 years old."

Young and Foolish

A young accountant, fresh out of college is being interviewed by the owner of a small business.

"I need someone with an accounting degree", says the business man. "But mainly I am looking for someone to do my worrying for me. I have lots of things to worry about, but I want someone else to worry about money matters."

"Interesting," says the interviewee. "How much are you offering?"

"You can start with $75,000 a year," says the owner.

"That's a great salary," says the young accountant. "How can a business like yours afford to pay so much?"

"That," says the business owner "is your first worry."

Parrots

An accountant goes into a pet shop to buy a parrot.

The shop owner shows him three parrots on a perch and says, "The parrot on the left costs $500."

"Why does the parrot cost so much?" - asked the accountant.

"Well," replies the owner. "It knows how to do complex audits."

The accountant then asks, "How much does the middle parrot cost?"

The owner replies, "That one costs $1000 because it can do everything that the first one can do, and it can also prepare detailed financial forecasts."

The stunned accountant asks about the third parrot, to be told that it will cost $4000 if he wants to buy it.

The startled accountant says, "That's expensive. Just what does that parrot do?"

The owner replies, "Well, I have never seen him do a darn thing at all, but the other two do call him Senior Partner."

The Train Ride

Three accountants and three auditors are about to board a train to a convention. As they were standing in line for tickets, the auditors noticed that the accountants bought only one ticket between them.

The auditors bought their three tickets and boarded the train but watched the accountants to see how they were going to manage with only one ticket.

As soon as the train left the station, the three accountants moved from their seats and they all squeezed into one restroom.

Soon the conductor came through the carriage and knocked on the restroom door saying "Ticket please." The door was opened slightly and an arm reached out and the one ticket was handed to the ticket collector.

The next day, the auditors decided to do the same thing, so they only purchased one ticket between the three of them.

However they noticed the accountants didn't purchase any tickets at all.

They all boarded the train and as soon as the train left the station, the three auditors hurry for the restroom.

A few moments later, one of the accountants gets up from his seat, knocks on the restroom door and says, "Ticket please."

Easy Measurement

One sunny day, three accountants are standing near a tall pole and wondering about its height.

The first accountant, a CPA says, "I do not think there is any authoritative guidance on how to measure the height of a pole; that is not the job of accountants."

The second accountant, a professor at a state university says, "If we take a survey of similar locations and we asked people about the height of poles, then we should be able to deduce height of this pole, and we will get a good enough estimate of its height."

The third accountant, a professor at an Ivy League university confidently claims, "If we measure the shadow of the pole under different conditions, then I can run a multivariate regression model and will be able to give a very good estimate of the height."

An engineer overhears the conversation and as if he can help.

The accountants tell him that it is a complex problem, but politely ask for his opinion.

The engineer smiles, lifts the pole from the base, measures it, and says, "It is twelve feet and three inches."

The accountants all look at the engineer, laugh contemptuously and say in unison, "We wanted to know the height of the pole and he tells us the length."

Wife Or Mistress

An artist, an architect and an accountant were chatting about whether they preferred to spend time with the wife or with a mistress.

The artist told the others that he preferred spending time with his wife, as it helped them build a solid foundation for an enduring relationship.

The architect said that he preferred spending time with his mistress, as he found the passion and mystery of a mistress intoxicating.

The accountant said, "I like both."

"Both?" the others queried.

The accountant explained, "Yes. Because if you have both a wife and a mistress, they will each assume that you are spending time with the other woman, and so you can go into the office in peace and get plenty of work done."

Long Division

A 57-year-old accountant is frustrated with his sex life.

One day he leaves a letter at home for his wife which read: "I am 57 years old, and by the time you receive this letter I will be at the Imperial Hotel with my beautiful and sexy nineteen year old secretary."

When he arrived at the hotel, there was a letter waiting for him that read as follows:

"Dear husband, I am also 57 years old, and by the time you get this letter I will be at the Grand Hotel with my nineteen year old toy boy. Because you are an accountant, you will understand that 19 goes into 57 many more times than 57 goes into 19."

Armageddon Discussion

A young female accountant is sitting at the bar after work one night, when a large sweaty construction worker sits down next to her.

They begin talking and after a while the conversation moves on to nuclear war.

The accountant asks the construction worker, "If you hear the sirens go off, and you know you've only got twenty minutes left to live, what would you do?"

The construction worker replies, "I am going to jump on anything that moves."

The construction worker then asks the accountant what she would do to which she replies, "I'm going to keep perfectly still."

Train Passengers

An accountant, a lawyer, a beautiful lady, and an old woman were on a train, sitting 2x2 facing each other.

The train went into a tunnel and when the carriage went completely dark, a loud "smack" was heard.

When the train came out of the tunnel back into the light the lawyer had a red hand print on his face. He had been slapped on the face.

The old lady thought, "That lawyer must have groped the young lady in the dark and she slapped him."

The hottie thought, "That lawyer must have tried to touch me, got the old lady by mistake, and she slapped him."

The lawyer thought, "That accountant must have groped the hottie, she thought it was me, and slapped me."

The accountant sat there thinking, "I can't wait for another tunnel so I can slap that lawyer again!"

Bank Robbery

Two accountants are in a bank on their lunch break, when a gang of armed robbers burst in.

Several of the robbers line up the bank's customers, including the accountants, against a wall and proceed to take their wallets, phones, watches etc.

While this is happening, the senior accountant jams something into the junior accountant's hand.

Without looking down, the junior accountant asks, "What's this?"

The senior accountant replies, "It's that 20 bucks I owe you."

The Briefcase

Sitting in a compartment on a train one day was a tooth fairy, an expensive accountant and a cheap accountant.

On a table in their compartment was a briefcase that was full of bank notes.

When the train entered a tunnel, everything became dark.

When the train exited the tunnel and the lights came back on, the briefcase had gone.

Who took the briefcase?

Well, it's obvious really - it had to be the expensive accountant since there is no such thing as a tooth fairy or a cheap accountant.

The Old Accountant

An old man was an accounting manager at a construction company.

Every day when he came to the office, he would opening his desk drawer, study something in it very carefully and then close the drawer.

After twenty years working at the same position, one day he died.

After his funeral, his colleagues went to his office to check what was in his drawer.

They opened the drawer and on a piece of paper in bold letters was written: "Debit Left, Credit Right."

Business Ethics

An accountancy student asks a partner to explain ethics in accountancy.

The partner thinks for a moment and then says the following, "Mr Roberston, one of our clients, came to see me last week and paid his bill of $1,000 in cash. As he left I counted the notes and they came to $1,100."

The student said, "I see. The ethics question is: do I tell the client?"

"Wrong answer," said the accountant. "The question is do I tell my partner."

Getting on the Train

An accountant is at Grand Central train station in New York City.

He notices a machine with a sign saying, 'Put a dollar in the slot and the machine will tell you who you are and what your plans are.'

Curious, he puts a dollar inside the slot.

The machine speaks, "You're Bryan Mills from New York, an accountant, you are 5 feet 10 inches tall and you weigh 210 pounds. You're about to take the 2.30 train to Chicago."

The man is stunned by the accuracy of the machine, but he suspects some trickery.

He wanders off, puts on a hat to disguise himself and goes back to the machine and puts another dollar in the slot.

The machine declares, "You're Bryan Mills from New York, an accountant, you are 5 feet 10 inches tall and you weigh 210 pounds. You're about to take the 2.30 train to Chicago."

The accountant was puzzled how a machine could possibly know that, so he decided to buy a wig to try and trick the machine.

He bought a wig and a false mustache and went back to the machine and put another dollar in the slot.

The machine declares, "You're Bryan Mills from New York, an accountant, you are 5 feet 10 inches tall and you weigh 210 pounds. You're about to take the 2.30 train to Chicago."

The accountant was now furious, so he wandered off, disguised himself as a woman and came back and put another dollar in the slot.

The machine declares, "You're Bryan Mills from New York, an accountant, you are 5 feet 10 inches tall and you weigh 210 pounds and with your stupidity you have just missed the train!"

Just One Wish

An accountant is walking in the woods one day when he comes across an old lamp.

He picks it up, rubs it; a genie appears.

The genie says, "I am a very powerful genie capable of fulfilling your treasured wish. But just the one wish."

The accountant is an extremely caring individual and he pulls out a map and says, "Well, my dearest wish is that you solve the Arab-Israeli conflict."

The genie says, "That's a tough one. Those people have been fighting for many generations. Nobody has been able to come up with a lasting peaceful solution. I don't think I could solve that problem. You probably should make another wish."

The accountant is understanding and says, "OK. The IRS recently asked me to re-design their 1040 form so that everyone can understand it. Can you help me with that?"

There is a long silence and eventually the genie declares, "Let's have another look at that map."

Accounting Graduate

A young accounting graduate, fresh out of University and thinking he knows everything, applied for his first job.

At interview, the prospective employer asked him what starting salary he was looking for.

The graduate replied, "Oh, I was thinking around $100,000 a year, depending on the benefits package."

The potential employer replied, "Well, how does this sound? Six weeks annual leave, 20% superannuation, paid expenses to overseas conferences every year, home telephone calls reimbursed and a company car replaced every 20,000 miles, starting with a Mercedes convertible."

The graduate sat up straight and tried not to look excited as he said, "Wow. Are you kidding?"

The employer replied, "Yes. But you started it."

The Mafia Godfather

A Mafia Godfather and his attorney meet with his former accountant. The Godfather demands, "Where is the 3 million bucks you stole from me?"

The accountant does not answer.

The Godfather asks again, "Where is the 3 million bucks you embezzled from me?"

The attorney interrupts, "The man is a deaf mute and he cannot understand you, but I can interpret for you."

The Godfather says, "Well, ask him what he has done with my money."

The attorney, using sign language, asks the accountant where he has stashed the three million dollars is.

The accountant signs back, "I don't know what you are talking about."

The attorney interprets to the Godfather, "He says he doesn't know what you are talking about."

The Godfather pulls out a 9 millimeter pistol, puts it to the temple of the accountant, cocks the trigger and says, "Ask him again where my damn money is or I'll blow his brains out."

The attorney signs to the accountant, "He really wants to know where the money is."

The accountant signs back, OK, OK. The money is hidden in a black briefcase on the top shelf in my garage."

The Godfather asks, "Well, what did he say?"

The attorney interprets to the Godfather, "He says 'Go to hell, you just don't have the guts to pull the trigger.'"

Getting The Right Job Title

A woman asks her accountant for help with filing her taxes.

The accountant gets her name, address, social security number, etc. and then he asks her, "What is your occupation?"

The woman replies, "I'm a whore."

The accountant flinches and says, "No. We can't write that down. That is too vulgar. Let's rephrase that."

The woman says, "Well OK, I'm a prostitute."

The accountant says "No, that is still too coarse."

They both ponder the situation for a while, and then the woman suddenly announces, "I know - I'm a poultry farmer."

The accountant then asks, "What on earth does chicken farming have to do with being a prostitute?"

She replies, "It's simple really. I raised over a thousand cocks last year."

Three Daughters

A male accountant was talking to two of his friends about their daughters.

The first friend says, "I was cleaning my daughter's room the other day and I found a pack of cigarettes. I didn't even know she smoked."

The second friend says, "That's nothing. I was cleaning my daughter's room the other day and I found a half full bottle of vodka. I didn't even know she drank."

The accountant says, "That's nothing. I was cleaning my daughter's room the other day and I found a pack of condoms. I didn't even know she had a penis."

Job Application

A businessman was interviewing job applicants for a managerial position. He developed a simple test to help choose the most appropriate candidate.

He asked each applicant, "What is two plus two?"

The first interviewee was a journalist who answered, "Twenty-two."

The second was a social worker who said, "I don't know the answer but I'm very glad that we have the opportunity to discuss it."

The third applicant was an engineer.

He pulled out a slide rule and answered, "somewhere between 3.999 and 4.001."

Next came an attorney who stated, "in the case of Hoskins vs. the Department of the Treasury, two plus two was proven to be four."

Next came a day trader who said, "Two plus two? Are you buying or selling?"

Finally, the accountant was interviewed.

When he was asked what two plus two was, he got up from his chair, went over to the door, closed it, came back and sat down.

Leaning across the desk, he said in a low voice, "How much do you want it to be?"

He got the job.

Chapter 5: Accountant Pick-Up Lines

You are one cute tax deduction.

Nice assets.

You're not just another journal entry. You balance my books.

In my office, I.R.S stands for I'm Really Sexy.

Let's get fiscal.

Is this my pocket calculator or am I just pleased to see you?

I am great with figures.

You've got a lovely pair of W-2's.

Let's fill out a 1040 - you are a 10 and I'm a 40.

You SUTA my needs.

Let's take the money and run.

You can call me Bond...Municipal Bond.

I'm not a liability. Just look at my assets.

Technically, having sex with me is a charitable gift.

Can I demonstrate double entry to you?

After filing today, I learned I have quite a strong flexible spending account. Are you flexible?

Can you help me balance my sheets?

Are your assets temporarily or permanently restricted? I would spare no expense to un-restrict them.

May I test your internal controls?

Did you know that sex toys are deductible this year?

After I'm done with your assets you'll have to test for impairment.

Can I put my substance all over your form?

I'd love to take you home and retire those assets.

I think you may need some help to fit this projection in your inbox.

Those are the nicest ledgers I've seen this accounting period.

I'll show you my spreadsheets if you show me yours.

I think I could add some serious value to your account.

I am filing single, but am looking to file jointly.

Let me help you with that double entry.

I don't care if you're rich or poor because I will make your cash flow.

What are you doing tomorrow night? I'm accounting on taking you out.

My fixed assets are rock solid.

Your assets will make me deposit my capital contribution early.

You liquidate my heart.

I've been auditing your body, and it is in fine standing.

You can increase your charitable contributions by giving me your digits.

I am the accountant your mother warned you about.

How about we get out of here and appreciate each other's assets?

Let me withhold you.

You should take credit for what you do to my debit.

If I take you home, it'll be an experience you aren't going be writing off anytime soon.

What are you doing tomorrow night? Because I'm accounting on taking you out.

I won't be too taxing for you.

If I help you screw Uncle Sam, can I be next?

If I take you home, it will be an experience you aren't going to write off anytime soon.

Can I process some entries in the back office?

My feelings for you will never depreciate.

I'd do just about anything to see your GAAP.

You make my pants file for an extension.

Chapter 6: Bumper Stickers For Accountants

Accountants work their assets off.

Kiss an accountant. It's tax deductible.

I have a calculator, and I know how to use it.

Trust me. I am an accountant.

It's accrual world.

I am good with figures.

---

10 out of 9 accountants can't count.

Numbers don't lie – people do.

A good accountant is a debit to the profession.

No, being in the red is not a good thing.

A good accountant never makes misteaks.

I like to play with other people's money.

The best things in life are free - plus tax, of course.

I do it at month end.

Chapter 7: How Accountants Do It

Accountants do it by the book.

Accountants do it to the bottom line.

Accountants do it with double entries.

Accountants do it between spread sheets.

Accountants do it within the budget.

Accountants do it without losing their balance.

Accountants are certified to do it in public.

Chapter 8: Summary

Hey, that's pretty well it for this book. I hope you've enjoyed it.

I've written a few other joke books for other professions, and here are just a few sample jokes from my lawyers joke book:-

Definition of a lawyer: A person who only has an opinion once you pay them.

Q: What's grey and not there?

A: *A lawyer on vacation.*

Q: What does a lawyer use for birth control?

A: *His personality.*

About The Author

Chester Croker has written many joke books and has twice been named Comedy Writer Of The Year by the International Jokers Guild.

Chester is known to his friends as either Chester the Jester or Croker the Joker!

Chester's first ever job was as an accounts clerk, and he came across many interesting characters in the accounts department, which provided him with plenty of material for this joke book.

If you enjoyed the book, please leave a review on Amazon so that other accountants can have a good laugh too.

Thanks in advance.

The Final Word

The Four Laws of Accounting:

1. Trial balances don't.
2. Bank reconciliations never do.
3. Working capital does not.
4. Return on investment never will.

Printed by Amazon Italia Logistica S.r.l.
Torrazza Piemonte (TO), Italy

15969656R00062